I Was Wrong,
but
God Made Me Right!

Written by Frank Friedmann

Illustrated by "MOM" Friedmann

First Printing: 1997

ISBN # 0-9659319-0-0

Manufactured in the United States of America by IPC Printing
Baton Rouge, Louisiana

Living in Grace Publications: 10051 Siegen Lane
Baton Rouge, Louisiana 70810

Do you ever do bad things?
Do you ever say bad things?
Is it hard for you to stop saying
and doing bad things?

Do you think something
might be wrong with you?

If so, then you are about to
read some really good news....

Yes, there is something wrong with you!!!

So what's the good news?

The good news is that God does not want you to be wrong,
so He did something to make you right! Isn't that great?

Let's find out what God did for you!

The Bible tells us that we are earthen vessels (II Cor. 4:7),
which is a fancy word for clay pots—or cups.
All people are like cups, and that includes you.

Cups come in all kinds of sizes, shapes, and colors.
They may look different, but they are the same in a very important way.
They are all made to be filled with something good.

It is the same with people. We may look different on the outside,
but we were all made to be filled with something good on the inside.
We were made to be filled with God. That's why God made you.
He wants to be like a giant faucet to you,
so He can fill you with Himself (Eph. 3:19).

(Did you notice that there is no
handle to turn off God's faucet?
He always pours out to us.
Isn't that great?)

This is the way it was for Adam and Eve in the Garden of Eden.
God filled each of them so full of His life and love that
they overflowed with God's love to each other.
What a wonderful life they must have had.....

...until that terrible day when they listened to Satan and believed the lie that he told them. They believed that they would be happier if they filled their lives with things, instead of God.

When they tried to fill their lives with other things, they did wrong. But something else happened too. They became wrong and separated from God. Now they were like upside down cups. God could not fill them any more. Nothing could fill them. They were empty. They were wrong!

(This is the way it is for all people. Since we all come from Adam and Eve, we are all born wrong, empty, and separated from God. Romans 5:19)

People did not like to be wrong and empty, so they tried to make themselves right and full. They tried to fill their lives with toys, jewelry, clothes, and lots of other things. But nothing could fill them, because they were wrong.

(Did you see that God's faucet is still on? God wants to fill us, but we won't let Him.)

As the wrong and empty people tried to fill themselves full,
they became very selfish and wanted everything to be their way.
This selfishness caused hurt, anger, and fear as
they lied, stole, and fought with each other.

These things are called sins, and they are wrong.
People were not made to sin. They were made to enjoy
God and each other. But sin acts like a fence.
It keeps people from God, the only one who can truly fill them.
It also keeps people from each other. People had a problem...

...but God solved the problem. He sent Jesus to take away that "fence of sins" by dying on the cross. People can now be forgiven by believing in Jesus and what He did <u>for us</u> (Heb. 9:28).
That is good news!

With their sins taken away, people can get close to God again. But people needed more than that. Even though people were forgiven for doing wrong, there was still something wrong with them. They were like upside-down cups. They could not be filled. They needed to be made right.

God solved that problem, too. When Jesus died on the cross, God put all those people who believe in Jesus on the cross with Him. This was so they could die with Jesus (Gal. 2:20). Then God buried them with Jesus, and He made them alive again with Jesus as brand new and "RIGHT" people (Rom. 6:4-6, II Cor. 5:17). This is what God did <u>to us</u>, and that is great news!

(We cannot understand how God crucified us with Jesus 2,000 years ago. We were not even born yet! But God never told us to understand it. He just told us to believe it.)

Once again, people can be filled with God (Eph. 3:19).
But that's not the end of the truth!
God did even more for His people (Eph. 3:20).

After the people were made right, God came to live inside them.
He put the faucet of His own life inside each of them so He could fill
them full from the inside out (John 7:38).

Now people do not have to be empty. They can stop being selfish. They can love each other, because they are filled with God. He can fill them so full that they overflow to others. This is what Jesus wants to do <u>in</u> and <u>through</u> <u>us.</u> This is the greatest news, and it is called "The Gospel of Jesus Christ".

Sadly, not everyone believes in Jesus. Do you see the cups that are still upside down? These are the people who do not choose to believe in what Jesus did for them. They cannot get full, because they will not let Jesus make them right.
They are very unhappy. Isn't that sad?

God loves us very much. Even though all of us turned away from God,
He did not turn away from us. He gave His life for us on the cross.
He made us right again, so that He can live in us and always make
us full. What we need to do is believe Him and
thank Him for what He did (John 6:29).

This is the only way for us to be filled.
We need to live our lives His way, with Him living
inside us and filling us with His life.

Do you want your wrongs to be gone?
Do you want to be made right?
Do you want to be filled with God,
the way He made you to be?

Then talk to Him and pray this prayer:

Father, I agree with you that I have done wrong things in my life.
I also agree with you that I am wrong and need to be made right.

Thank you for sending Jesus to die for my sins.
Thank you for putting me on the cross with Jesus,
so that I could be made right.

Thank You for coming to live inside of me.
Please fill me up with Yourself,
so that I can overflow with Your love, Your kindness,
and Your joy to others. I trust You to do that for me,
in Jesus' name. Amen. **AMEN!!!**

Hooray! You are now right and Jesus lives inside you to fill you full!
From now on you must trust that He will be able to take care of you.
He may not give you whatever you want, but
He will give you whatever you need. This is
called "living" or "resting" in Jesus (John 15:1-5).

(We want toys and candy, but we need love, forgiveness and food.
Do you understand the difference?)

Please remember this great danger. You may try to fill yourself
with other things like you used to do, instead of trusting God to
fill you. As you learn to trust Him, do not expect to do it perfectly.
It will be a struggle, and sometimes you may fail to trust Him...

...but He is true. You can always trust Him. He will never leave you and He will never stop loving you. He will stay with you until the day He brings you home to live with Him forever in heaven.

He is your GOD and you are HIS CHILD!
That is really good news, isn't it? <u>Yes, it is.</u>

Thank you, Jesus.

This book is dedicated to the Lord Jesus Christ,
in respect and with thanksgiving
for His Person and Work.

With thanks to all my friends in Christ, who
offered their assistance in editing and ideas.
You know who you are, and you are great.

Special thanks to John Russin and Brett Brooks, for their
free flowing red pens, which called me to
communicate in the childlike manner
in which I seek to live.

For further information regarding conferences, audio tapes, and other publications from Living in Grace, please write to:

Living in Grace
10051 Siegen Lane
Baton Rouge, LA. 70810
or call
(504)769-8844; or
(800) 484-2046 ext. 9506

(To order   SPECIAL INTRODUCTORY   r book;
                         PRICE - $4.95

Call for our multiple purchase discount.

LIVING IN GRACE

"Leading people to the Grace of God,
the Person of Jesus Christ,
who sets men free indeed!"